I0420664

Black Bird Ops:

A Super Hero Manual Book

by

Daniel K. Arnold

Black Bird Ops:

A Super Hero Manual Book

Chapter 1

This may be a new tale for you. Have you ever met someone really out of it?

Have you ever met a person going on an adventure in his/her own head?

Meet the realm of Black Bird Ops—introduced in the small companion book, Everchanging. He's real, yet he's a façade. He's this Super Hero's favorite delusion.

And he's going "undercover." Some call him a night owl. Typically, he won't wear sunglasses unless the mission calls for it.

He believes he's an American hero, but at times it's a façade to boost his hurting self-esteem.

Black Bird Ops absorbs any information leading him to sound

more trendy and real. He dreams of being a special agent and wonder if he's already been recruited.

He is deluded in this persona and partially under the confusion of satan.

Black Bird Ops, the character of schizoaffective, originated from 'normalcy' and evolved to Mister Energy Plus. Finally, after enough stress Black Bird Ops became my coping mechanism.

As I talked about semi-sensitive governmental terminology, I began to relive the seemingly covert world in my sleep.

Black Bird Ops:

A Super Hero Manual Book

Chapter 2

There is no logical explanation for the origins of this Super Hero gone Black Bird Ops! I can only attempt to piece together Schizoaffective for the world through a diagnosis that is Bipolar with paranoid Schizophrenic features.

During the day, this persona does not usually come out.

At night, it feels natural for this character to want to be productive as it is sleepless and lonely.

Help me oh Lord to overcome Black Bird Ops. I need help!

Studies have shown the insomnia side of Abilify and that plays a part in the adventure.

Abilify is a part of Black Bird Ops's arsenal without choice. Because

Abilify is now injected into the Super Hero, the description of Abilify implants in his legs seems appropriate.

Not everyone who is Schizoaffective takes Abilify, therefore Black Bird Ops's description in this book may seem somewhat unique and that leaves the character ever eager to reach out to others.

Black Bird Ops is fascinated by similar characters like Deep Skull but at the same time they have a tendency to scare him.

Delusions are not cool no matter how glamorous they seem.

Black Bird Ops you need to leave in the name of Jesus!

Black Bird Ops:

A Super Hero Manual Book

Chapter 3

I live my days with a semblance of sanity. Few know of my secret night life except other cronies. It's a "dog eat dog eat dog world out there."

Who can you trust under the guise of the night?

It's nighttime and this night is atypical.

I did not wake up every hour on the hour with fearful night terror hallucinations.

Instead, I had a normal dream and woke up after 2am thankful for a semblance of sanity.

Thank you Jesus.

No bugs, mice, poop delusions of things in my pants.

Nope, just peace.

Thank you Jesus. He told me I would get more sleep. I am thankful now for therapy because I badly need it.

I am on a blood-work fast for twelve hours now and I want me some comfort food!

I want some soda in the fridge. I want some sort of "creature comfort."

Oh, it is life. I will wait for correct labs because I need to get better.

Black Bird Ops:

A Super Hero Manual Book

Chapter 4

I've tested the effects of cutting out the medication Abilify many times.

I insist on going against the medical consensus.

As Mister Energy Plus I can be a real rebel and as Black Bird Ops I can get real desperate. Together, they make a one-of-a-kind shifting persona.

Black Bird Ops you have to leave, but I am tempted to keep a little Mister Energy Plus buzz in my steps.

Normal doesn't always seem that appealing.

"Welcome to the Super Hero life of relying on God and eachother."

Black Bird Ops:

A Super Hero Manual Book

Chapter 5

I have the urge to write, but my body is fatigued. It is 5:40am and I am riding on the bus around Lansing, Michigan, USA.

Yawn.. "Good Morning America." Slowly getting up.

Praise the Lord. I am thankful for a hero like Ricky who reminded me to follow the Holy Spirit.

This ride is bumpy and I don't have a lot on my mind. Yet, I am thankful for my family, friends, God and readership.

God Bless you all!

God Bless the suffering right now. God Bless those out on the streets with sleepless nights. God Bless the beggars and those in pain.

God Bless the needy and abused over and over again. Rescue them from "harm's way" and show them your love oh God.

Have mercy on the brokenhearted and the ones that cannot defend themselves. Reach out to the meek and lowly. Grant them peace, forevermore.

You see I just had a little tiny bitter taste. I have not suffered again and again like others.

And my eternity is glory land if I should so continue in God's kindness.

Lord, have mercy on the suffering. Lord, restore what was lost.

Help us all to forgive in the name of Jesus, Amen.

Let us pray as Jesus demonstrated on the cross at Calvary: "Lord forgive them for they know not what they do."

Black Bird Ops:

Chapter 6

Have you ever been severely wronged and the incident was swept under the rug?

We must learn to forgive yet take action when necessary.

Justice is tricky business. For we are expected to act justly despite what anyone else does. There is only room to keep one's own integrity and remember:

"Vengeance is mine saieth the Lord."

We cannot take matters into our own hands, but we can take a course of action to protect ourselves.

In my situation, I was a whistleblower. I filled boxes with complaints that were ignored in their abundance.

I was a real button-pusher. Why? Because I'm a natural written creative communicator. I like to see my thoughts on paper and get the message out.

If I have input, I am determined to get results.

What am I to do when I really need justice? I assumed tell everyone in authority until someone reacts.

Wrong.

The proper answer is logical. Go through the chain of commands.

Pray to God and go to the most immediate person in authority.

After praying, contact the Recipient Rights Office most proximate to the location of the rights violation.

Next, do not give up on appeals.

<u>Always</u> forgive!

Never stop learning and teaching others from what you learn from your difficult experiences.

Put everything in God's hands and move on.

Do not let an incident hold you back back from your future. Finally, do not withhold justice when others are being harmed.

Forgiveness is difficult. Sometimes justice must be left in the hands of God.

Black Bird Ops:

A Super Hero Manual Book

Chapter 7

Door (A) is closed.

Door (B) is opening.

There is hope for you and for me. We are blessed. When Option #1 is no longer an option, do not sweat it!

God may be opening a door to your destiny that "no man can shut!"

I believed I was meant to be a school teacher. I did not know when I failed teacher internship that there were other options left.

It seemed like the end of the line, but God had other plans.

"Plans to prosper me and not to harm me, plans to give me a hope and a future (Bible)."

Now I write books and edit newsletters. God is on the move and He'll use you if you'll let Him. Do not let go of Plan (B) when and if Plan (A) fails. Move down the line until you find the right one.

It took multiple tries for Einstein to find the right light bulb configuration. The same goes true for life at times!

Black Bird Ops:

A Super Hero Manual Book

Chapter 8

Q: When is enough, enough?

A: The day I die.

I will not be satisfied unless I productively make something of myself day after day.

If you've written a good poem, do not stop there. Write more the next day. Be consistent. "Finish what you start."

Create a legacy.

Super Heroes exist in part to inspire others. Do some good works. Make a difference for Jesus. Be real in this lifetime.

Discipleship is a great way to do this. One by one, student by student. Investment instead of scattershot.

Breakthrough lesson learned. Change can happen today by the power of God.

Be an inspiration to someone else a few steps behind you on the journey.

Do not be afraid to reach out to motivated individuals older, younger, or the same age as you.

Imagine having other Super Heroes tutored by you accompanied by their own unique giftings.

Perhaps, they have a thing or two to teach you too! This is inspired by God. "Bear one another's burdens."

Love at all times. Never give up on life. We are blessed!

Black Bird Ops:

A Super Hero Manual Book

Chapter 9

Super Heroes need extra space to compensate for their, shall we say, idiosyncrasies. Not everyone shares the same place. This is true of Black Bird Ops.

A person of his/her inkling enjoys his own space while simultaneously being codependent.

Go figure.

This means he wants freedom, but the ability to use others' space when convenient.

Imagine the anger of having your place trashed for the enjoyment of the co-dependent Super Hero.

Every character is unique, especially among Super Heroes, because God made no two the same.

How do we cope with this monstrocity—communication, forgiveness and love?

They go a long way in building and maintaining relationships.

It is not proper to abruptly write people off—unless they try to burn down the house or spur on a police call.

Even there, there is a place for letting go, starting over, and saying, "I will be one of this guy or gal's few friends," like Jesus.

"Whatsoever you do unto the least of these brethren, you do unto me."

Be Jesus to the spiritually blind. Let your life give them eyes to see.

Black Bird Ops:

A Super Hero Manual Book

Chapter 10

Squeezing turnips. Asking for something when nothing is there. Not being realistic. "Kicking him now that he's down."

Sometimes Super Heroes are too depleted to move a muscle.

Sometimes Super Heroes fake this because they choose to.

Reality hurts, but at times pain is good. Pain can be a motivator. Pain as punishment can turn a sinner from his/her wicked ways.

Do not be afraid to inflict a little pain, but be mindful of the weakened sickness of the Super Hero.

A man who is depressed may not have the strength to move and a depleted angry OCD person may be extremely bothered finding deposits not his own in his place of dwelling.

When Ice Man meets Mister Energy Plus in the middle of the night (Black Bird Ops) for confrontation, look out!

Both now have little patience. Ice Man has energy because of his anger.

Black Bird Ops is in emergency crash mode talking like a private eye detective.

Fireworks may ensue and it might be a good time to wait until morning for the storm to clear.

Otherwise, the exchange may become unforgettable!

In short, make big allowances for Super Heroes as you have not walked in their enormous or teeny shoes.

Black Bird Ops:

A Super Hero Manual Book

Chapter 11

Morning America. I am sleepy. I chose to wake up early. I mean to stay awake. Life is full of decisions moment by moment that add up.

This is true of the typical Super Hero diet. Some grab excessive caffeine like Mister Energy Plus. Others grab beer after beer to try to get some cheer (or simply go to sleep).

And it seems to work for the moment. As blocks of dependency are built upon dependency, an addictive tendency seems to commence in many Super Heroes.

Call it self-medicating, but much of the Super Hero populations seems irresponsible in substance intake to cope with the pain they are facing.

What seems like idiosyncrasies actually shortens life. It's reality. Where's the solution?

Turn from your sin seems to be the too simple answer for the suffering Super Hero.

A little sensitivity, compassion and peer support goes a long way.

Sometimes you have to have been there to have the empathy to understand.

Yet, everyone has the capacity to love, listen, and extend forgiveness.

And point out those epic qualities that make Super Heroes super!

Black Bird Ops:

A Super Hero Manual Book

Chapter 12

I am blessed, but sometimes I am ashamed. Not everyone believes in my receiving lifestyle. I am told SSI will not last. I am told to get a job and stop faking it.

Let me tell you, four books and twenty-five pages of newsletters later, I am not here to play around.

I have a message and a destiny.

I am purposeful and I am not giving up. I have suffered burn out, but my heart is very much alive.

I desire to see breakthrough in my life and yours.

I t is not the place of a non-physician to judge whether someone is able to work. This is between a person and his/her doctor.

Writing is my job. It is no more dignified than any other work and no less despite having no paycheck to show for it.

I'm thankful for God's provision and aim to give back to society through writing.

Black Bird Ops:

A Super Hero Manual Book

Chapter 13

They say, "There is no free lunch," but in Lansing God provides. He's there for people when they are not there for themselves.

Salvation Army, Volunteers of America, the nicknamed "Chocolate Milk Church" to name a few.

God provides out of the service and pockets of others. We should be grateful as a society for what we are provided and not ashamed or judging.

"The rain falls on the good and bad alike."

Do not give up on reaching out no matter what position you are in in society. The job needs to get done regardless.

"Love at all times." "If at all possible, be at peace with everyone."

Reach the unreachable with simple orchestrated or unorchestrated acts of kindness.

Love with sincerity for our attitudes can be read. Motive shines out of the heart attitude.

Be unique. Love your enemies. Do good to them that persecute you. Never let up. Show mercy like Jesus.

When you serve, your breakthrough is just around the corner.

<u>Black Bird Ops:</u>

<u>A Super Hero Manual Book</u>

Chapter 14

Dreams do not come true overnight—necessarily. Have faith in God to move mountains in your time of need.

While you tarry, give thanks to God for everything. "God works out all things to the good of those that love God and are called according to His purpose."

Be faithful. Breakthrough comes at an unknown timing. When seeking breakthroughs it is important to seek out eternal treasure rather than simply material success.

We are told in the Bible that "We will reap a harvest if we don't give up."

This harvest can be described as legacy. Some people do not see the difference they've made until after-life. Eternal reward is great reward.

I go on to say vision must be carried out if it is of the Lord. All the powers in Hell cannot prevail against it. Success will happen, though not always seen with the naked eye.

"I can do all things through Christ who strengthens me."

This is a vision for him/her who believes. Do not let go of it. We all need to live as we are leaving a legacy.

People are famished in many different ways. They need our inspiration that comes from God.

Be a light as He is a light.

Watch the darkness flee.

Wahooo!

Be led by the Spirit and make a difference in your sphere of influence.

If you are a painter, paint.
If you are a talker, talk the truth.

If you smile and encourage, don't
give up when the going gets tough!

People are listening, reading, talking,
thinking. Be an inspiration.

Black Bird Ops:

A Super Hero Manual Book

Chapter 15

Super Heroes are human. They sin on purpose. It is no accident. They commit willful sin with the knowledge of the truth-- living like they do not know better.

Sowing to the flesh is death and Super Heroes are without excuse.

Now is the time to pick up our feet again. The hour of repentance is here!

"Seek Him while He may be found. Call on Him while He is near."

Now is the time to turn our hearts back to God—to begin living the abundant life. For sin does not satisfy but for a moment.

And, then an empty condemning feeling is all that is left.

Let us leave this pattern of transgression and turn to the Lord. Let us learn to live 100% for God and God alone.

The past is the past. Be free. Repent and return to Jesus. Let us live a new life—a free life a happy life.

"Blessed is he who does not walk in the counsel of the ungodly, nor standeth in the way of sinners, nor sit in the seat of scoffers (Psalm 1:1)."

It is time to clear the runway for Jesus. Let us walk a straight path and associate with men and women who follow Him. Let us take the time to rest and the time to walk.

Let us serve wholeheartedly.

And zoom to the horizon as Super Heroes.

Black Bird Ops:

A Super Hero Manual Book

Chapter 16

If you cannot play the music, let someone gifted take the lead in that department.

Do not be a showboat; be a humble inspiration.

Look to Jesus first and humble people second. Find inspiration and know that people are imperfect.

People let us down, but God will never let us down.

"God demonstrates His love for us in this, while we were yet sinners, Christ died for us."

We can find people nonetheless who are great examples, great inspirers, great livers of the faith.

"Without faith it is impossible to please Him."

I am waiting on the Lord for a miracle-- change in my life.

Yet I must take action. I must live out by faith and take a step of faith.

"With God all things are possible."

Black Bird Ops:

A Super Hero Manual Book

Chapter 17

We have been entrusted with some. Let us be faithful with some. For God gives the increase.

God can and will make a good mountain out of a good molehill.

So "run the race as to get the prize."

Your breakthrough is on its way. What do we live for?

Our answer should be to love God and others. Everything else falls into place.

"Seek first the Kingdom of God and His righteousness and all these things shall be added unto you."

God brings the increase when we seek Him first.

SideNote: Right now my head is sweating, my head is pounding and I'm concerned about manic symptoms.

Yet I know, God is in control and bringing my dream to pass as we speak.

Today, I am more motivated than yesterday. I am dreaming for my future. I see God at the center of it.

"For I know the plans I have for you, plans to prosper you and not to harm you, plans to give you hope and a future."

God cares about my future and can use "bad news" for His purpose.

With God's impact upon even dire circumstances, tragedies can actually turn into breakthrough through God's broken people—Super Heroes.

You may not realize it, but you are a Super Hero. Even if you are diagnosed mentally ill and looked down upon by society, you matter.

You are crucial. You are needed for society to function. God makes all the difference in marginalized lives and seemingly ideal lives.

God wants us to continue in His kindness, serve Him and be faithful.

Faithfulness reaps a harvest if we do not give up.

Your moment of breakthrough is now. A changed mind is a changed life by the power of God.

Saul changed his mind and became Paul. Abram changed his mind and became Abraham.

These new people were appointed new identities by God—applying their past to change the world.

The past is over, but its applications are not forgotten. Your calling begins now, but was created by God long before. Get excited!

Black Bird Ops:

A Super Hero Manual Book

Chapter 18

What do we look for in change? Do we elicit it in others or go about it in our own lives first?

We need to look at our own selves with a microscope before studying others flaws.

Let the little things pass to make room for new things.

It seems that I cannot write now, but God knows what He is doing.

He created me. He created you for a purpose.

It is time to move forward. Praise the Lord. We can do this with each other and with God!

"I waited for the Lord on high and He heard my cry. He pulled me out of the miry and set me feet upon a rock."

I know breakthrough is here and will continue to come. We are victors!

www.ingramcontent.com/pod-product-compliance
Lightning Source LLC
Chambersburg PA
CBHW061804280526
45787CB00003BA/1480

9781519257253